For the Teacher

This reproducible study guide consists of instructional material to use in conjunction with a specific novel. Written in chapter-by-chapter format, the guide contains a synopsis, pre-reading activities, vocabulary and comprehension exercises, as well as extension activities to be used as follow-up to the novel.

NOVEL-TIES are either for whole class instruction using a single title or for group instruction where each group uses a different novel appropriate to its reading level. Depending upon the amount of time allotted to it in the classroom, each novel, with its guide and accompanying lessons, may be completed in two to four weeks.

The first step in using NOVEL-TIES is to distribute to each student a copy of the novel and a folder containing all of the duplicated worksheets. Begin instruction by selecting several pre-reading activities in order to set the stage for the reading ahead. Vocabulary exercises for each chapter always precede the reading so that new words will be reinforced in the context of the book. Use the questions on the chapter worksheets for class discussion or as written exercises.

The benefits of using NOVEL-TIES are numerous. Students read good literature in the original, rather than in abridged or edited form. The good reading habits formed by practice in focusing on interpretive comprehension and literary techniques will be transferred to the books students read independently. Passive readers become active, avid readers.

Novel-Ties® are printed on recycled paper.

SYNOPSIS

The story begins on a cold October morning in Monument, Massachusetts. The narrator explains that he is riding to Vermont to visit his father. The speaker recounts that he left home secretly, bringing only his small savings, a gift for his father, warm clothes, and his father's old woolen cap. He alludes to Amy Hertz, the zany girl whom he loves and misses, a bottle of pills emptied into the sink, and the fear that he is being followed.

This terrifying story consists of a boy's account of his bicycle trip interwoven with transcripts of a dialogue between "T" and "A"; the identity of "T" is not revealed until the shocking climax, but it slowly becomes evident that "A" is "Adam," the boy on the bike, who is in an institution. "T" claims to be helping "A" fill in the many memory gaps he has about his past, but "A" is suspicious of "T's" motives. Yet, he wants to determine his own identity and how he came to be at the institution. Despite his drug-induced confusion, he begins to remember that something significant happened when he was four years old. He overheard a tense discussion between his parents; then experienced a frightening bus ride in which the family moved to a new home. From that time on, his formerly exuberant, affectionate parents became anxious and reclusive.

On his journey, the boy stops at a gas station where he meets a kind, elderly man who gives him a map. The boy tells the man that he is making the seventy-mile trip to see his father, who is in a hospital in Rutterburg, Vermont.

In the next tape transcript, "T" questions "A" about Paul Delmonte and Amy Hertz. "A" becomes confused and upset, ending the interview abruptly.

As he bikes, the boy sings "The Farmer in the Dell," a favorite song from his childhood. As he reminisces about bantering with his father, we learn that the boy's name is "Adam Farmer." With muscles aching, he continues riding uphill and is nearly attacked by a terrifying dog.

Although increasingly distrustful of Brint (the individual referred to as "T"), "A" divulges some of the "clues" he is beginning to remember. He mentions an episode in which his father, apparently avoiding someone, took him into the woods where they were attacked by a dog.

Tired and nauseated from his ride, Adam tries to telephone Amy, but no one answers the phone. Adam remembers how he and Amy met, colliding with arms full of books at the library entrance. Ebullient Amy drew him into her crazy schemes such as filling up shopping carts and then deserting them in the grocery aisles. Despite their closeness, Adam could never share his fears with her.

He now recalls how he secretly investigated his father's papers and discovered his name on two birth certificates each with a different birthdate. He also eavesdropped on a phone conversation between his mother and an aunt, which revealed the lie that his father had always told when he stated that the family had no relatives.

Meanwhile, Adam bikes through the rain and stops at a small restaurant where he is taunted by some local toughs, who follow him in a car and force him into a ditch. When he regains consciousness, he becomes aware of an elderly man who offers him a ride to the next town.

During the next interrogation, "A" talks about "the gray man," a vague character who visited the family periodically. Adam recalls that when he finally confronted his parents about the secrets they were keeping, they explained that the man was a government agent in charge of assigning new identities for the family and that Adam's father had once been a journalist, who had given testimony against the mob. After several murder attempts on the family, they had been given new names and were moved to Massachusetts, where the father was given a cover job as an insurance salesman.

Meanwhile, on the journey, Adam's bicycle is stolen, and a repulsive, obese man tells him where to find it. Adam finds the courage to grab his bike from the thief. He learns to his dismay that the motel he remembers his family visited the year before has long been deserted.

"A" calls his interrogator to reveal what he remembers. In a chilling finale, Adam tells his interrogator about the phone call his mother had received, how the family's cover might have been discovered, and how as a consequence, the family packed up for a "vacation." While the three were pausing at a reststop, a car plowed into them, killing Adam's mother and father.

It is finally clear that Adam has never been on an actual journey. In fact, during all this time, he has never left the institution. All of the characters he thought he met along the way were others who lived or worked at the institution. With many questions left unanswered, the story closes with a horrifying, revealing "advisory" by the (government) investigators. Although the "gray man" was probably responsible for betraying the family, he did such an efficient cover-up that he should be reinstated. Since the boy is the only living link to information his father had about the criminal organization, it is suggested that the boy should be "terminated."

PRE-READING ACTIVITIES

1. Preview the book by looking at the title, the author's name, and the illustration on the cover of the book. What do you think the book will be about? What are the words of the old children's song, "The Farmer in the Dell"? What could it mean to be "the cheese"? Have you read any other novels by Robert Cormier? If so, what is the general mood of his stories? Does he tend to have a positive or negative view of the world? Why do you think his novels are so popular?

2. With other students in your class, discuss whether anyone ever ran away from home. If so, what was the typical age for running away, what were the reasons for leaving and how did the journey end?

3. What does the word "interrogation" mean to you? Which word seems to have a more negative connotation—"question" or "interrogate"? Have you ever seen, read about, or even experienced an interrogation? Who was asking questions? Why? In what tone? Who was the subject? What was his or her reaction? If the subject supplied information, what happened to him or her? Did the questioning ever help the subject?

4. **Cooperative Learning Activity:** work in cooperative learning groups to discuss how you would deal with the following hypothetical situation:

   > Your parents have been lying to you about your identity. How would you feel? Whom would you tell? What could you do to uncover the secret in your past? What problems would you face?

   A Recorder in each group should summarize the discussion and present it orally to the class.

5. Do some research to learn about amnesia. What are its causes and treatments? What role does the therapist often take in the treatment of amnesia? What reactions might the client have to the "blanks" in memory, and to returning memories?

6. What is the technique of flashback that is often used in films, television, and literature? Where have you seen flashback used? Why is this technique used? Has it ever confused you? As you read this novel notice how flashback is used.

7. Read and become familiar with the psychological terms in the glossary on the following page. They will help you understand Adam's plight.

GLOSSARY OF PSYCHOLOGICAL TERMS

amnesia	complete or partial loss of memory
anxiety reaction	state of apprehension or fear
defense	keeping painful ideas repressed or out of awareness
free association	letting ideas flow uninterruptedly; a technique a therapist may use to uncover hidden memories
psychiatric profiles	written outlines based on a psychiatrist's evaluation of one's mental state
psychological residue	uncovered memories still existing within the mind
recapitulating	mentally reliving a previous experience
reflecting	responding technique in which a therapist, in an attempt to help the individual reach self-insight, avoids providing answers and repeats what the individual has said
paranoia	mental disorder characterized by delusions in which the subject imagines being threatened by others
resistance	individual's opposition to the therapist's attempts to help him or her remember something painful
trauma	shocking experience that has a lasting effect on one's mental life
withdrawal	retreat from thinking or talking about a given subject

PAGES 1 – 11 [Laurel-Leaf edition]

Vocabulary: Draw a line from each word on the left to its meaning on the right. Then use the numbered words to fill in the blanks in the sentences below.

1. warped		a.	afraid of enclosed spaces
2. claustrophobic		b.	indicating good or evil to come
3. resolute		c.	force of movement
4. omen		d.	bent out of shape
5. momentum		e.	hesitantly; done as through it were a trial
6. tentatively		f.	withdrew
7. retreated		g.	firmly decided

. . . .

1. The witness to the murder answered each question _____ because the violence of the crime hindered her memory.

2. The new student was _____ about taking the physics course even though he was warned of its difficulty.

3. The drawers of the oak dresser became _____ after being stored in a damp cellar.

4. After I jumped off the treadmill, I still felt the _____ of the moving belt.

5. The dark clouds and gathering winds were a(n) _____ of an approaching storm.

6. Because of his _____ tendencies, George avoided all elevators.

7. Jane _____ into silence when asked embarrassing questions about her family.

Questions:

1. When and where does the story take place? How does the weather reflect the narrator's inner state?

2. What suggests that the narrator is not on an ordinary bike trip?

Pages 1 – 11 (cont.)

3. What are "A's" memories? What are the gaps in his memory? How do these gaps make him feel? How does "Brint" respond to "A's" pauses?

4. What are "A's" feelings about Brint?

Questions for Discussion:

1. If you were in "A's" position, how would you regard Brint? How much would you reveal?

2. What connections can be made between the story told in the opening section and the transcribed therapy session which follows?

Literary Device: Point of View

Point of view in literature refers to the person telling the story. In a third-person narrative the author tells the story; in a first-person narrative one of the characters tells the story.

From whose point of view is the first section told?

_____

From whose point of view is the transcribed therapy session told?

_____

Why do you think the author switched points of view? Do you think this is helpful or confusing?

_____

_____

_____

Writing Activity:

Write about one of your earliest memories. Describe the incident and tell why you think it has remained in your memory. How old were you when the event occurred? Do you think your memory might be colored by what someone said or by a photograph that was shown to you?

_____

Pages 1 – 11 (cont.)

Literary Element: Characterization

The characters of the narrator, Amy, and Brint are revealed slowly as you read the book. Begin to fill in the character webs below with the facts or words of description that you think best tell about these characters. Compare your pertinent facts with those your classmates chose. As you read the book, continue to add to the web and make changes where necessary.

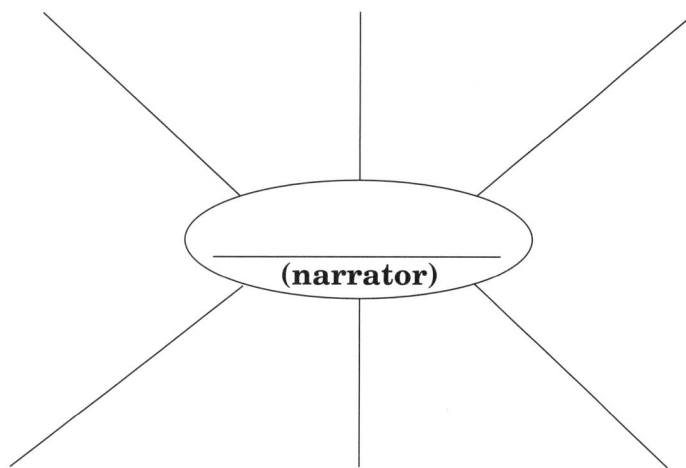

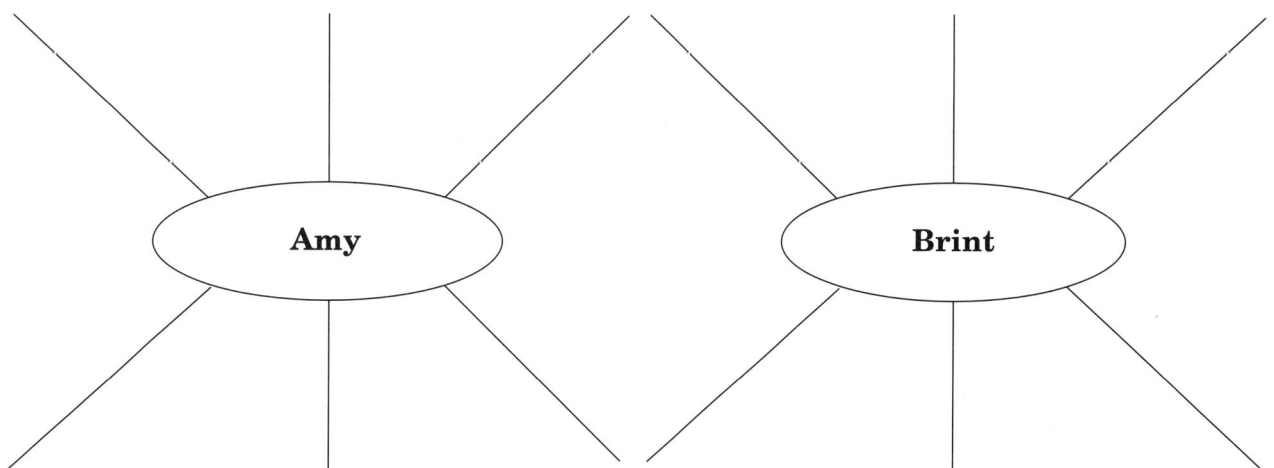

(narrator)

Amy

Brint

PAGES 12 – 24

Vocabulary: Synonyms are words with similar meanings. Draw a line from each word in column A to its synonym in column B. Then use the words in column A to fill in the blanks in the sentences below.

<u>A</u>

1. insignificant
2. raucously
3. vulnerable
4. impaled
5. hurtling
6. administered
7. obliterating

<u>B</u>

a. gave
b. pierced
c. speeding
d. defenseless
e. destroying
f. loudly
g. unimportant

. . . .

1. The team at mission control sat calmly as the space capsule was _____ through space.

2. The nurse _____ the vaccine to those who waited in line.

3. Although the results of the exam seemed _____ at first, they later proved to be important.

4. The tyrant was systematically _____ all written history of the former democratic government.

5. The young audience responded _____ to the slapstick comedy routine.

6. The marshmallow was _____ on a stick to toast it over the campfire.

7. Without any weapon, he felt _____ to attack from his enemies.

Questions:

1. Why does the narrator stop at the gas station?

2. What subjects does "A" prefer not to discuss? How does Brint respond?

3. What memories does the narrator associate with the song he sings?

Pages 12 – 24 (cont.)

4. How is the narrator's name revealed?

5. Why is Adam glad he did not take the pills?

Questions for Discussion:

1. Can you think of a song that would evoke childhood memories for you?

2. Describe Adam's out-of-body experience. What are some possible explanations for Adam's uneasiness?

Cooperative Learning Activity:

Divide your class into cooperative learning groups consisting of four or five students. Each group should assign one student the role of recorder as you discuss the meaning of the heading, "Tape Ozkooz 1430 date deleted T-A." Try to come to a consensus about its significance. Then appoint another member of each group to present the findings of the group to the rest of the class.

Writing Activity:

Adam realizes that by imagining that he is somewhere else, outside of himself, he can forget something that is troubling him. Pretend that you are Adam and write an entry in your journal. Describe one of your imaginary journeys and then (using clues from the story) explain what it is that you are trying to forget.

PAGES 25 – 43

Vocabulary: Use the context to determine the meaning of the underlined word in each of the following sentences. Then compare your definition with a dictionary definition.

1. He threw the frisbee <u>askew</u>, and commented, "Another crooked throw!"
   Your definition _____
   Dictionary definition _____

2. It is <u>futile</u> to try to escape from a maximum security prison.
   Your definition _____
   Dictionary definition _____

3. Their <u>camaraderie</u> was put to the test when each was asked to sign the document in blood as proof of their friendship.
   Your definition _____
   Dictionary definition _____

4. Although most people would fear being <u>marooned</u> on a desert island, I would actually enjoy being isolated from the rest of the world for a while.
   Your definition _____
   Dictionary definition _____

5. As she stared at the <u>apparition</u> in the doorway, the figure exclaimed, "You look as if you've seen a ghost!"
   Your definition _____
   Dictionary definition _____

Questions:

1. Compare Adam's encounter with the dog on the highway, with his earlier confrontation with the dog in the woods. How is each dog described? How does Adam escape from each situation?

2. How does Brint respond to Adam's questions about Brint and the hospital?

3. How does Adam analyze his own distrust of Brint? Why doesn't Adam decide to withhold all information?

4. How does Adam's image of his father change during the encounter with the dog?

Pages 25 – 43 (cont.)

5. What is Adam's physical and emotional state when he reaches Howard Johnson's?

6. In what passages does Adam's sense of time or space seem distorted?

Questions for Discussion:

1. Why do you think Adam's father dragged him into the woods? Do you think Adam really knows why? What do you think Adam doesn't know and what is he deliberately not telling Brint?

2. Do you think Adam's misgivings about Brint are justified?

3. Has there ever been an incident through which you glimpsed an unexpected side of one of your own parents?

Literary Device: Simile

A simile is a figure of speech in which two unlike objects are compared using the words "like" or "as." For example, Adam recalls that the dog had "eyes like marbles."

What is being compared?

_____

How does this make you feel about the dog?

_____

Write another simile describing the dog's eyes that would convey an opposite feeling.

_____

Writing Activity:

Imagine that you are Adam and the telephone call you want to make is able to go through. Write a short dialogue based upon what you know about Adam and Amy that would record this imaginary long-distance conversation.

PAGES 44 – 66

Vocabulary: Use the context to determine the synonym for the underlined word in each of the following sentences. Circle the letter of the word you choose.

1. In order to insure the ring, the jeweler was <u>appraising</u> the value of the diamond.
   a. assailing   b. rationalizing   c. assessing   d. subtracting

2. In an <u>exuberant</u> mood after learning of his award, the graduate hugged his mother.
   a. nonchalant   b. obscure   c. melancholy   d. enthusiastic

3. The stench from the garbage dump <u>assailed</u> our nostrils.
   a. attacked   b. appraised   c. rationalized   d. obscured

4. Grandmother's <u>lucid</u> childhood memories gave us a vivid image of her past.
   a. enthusiastic   b. obscure   c. nonchalant   d. clear

5. The driving directions to the seashore were so <u>vague</u> that we soon became lost.
   a. melancholy   b. unclear   c. unenthusiastic   d. lucid

Questions:

1. How does Adam describe Amy?
2. According to Adam, how has his mother changed?
3. What is the "Number"? How does Adam feel about participating in Amy's "Numbers"?
4. What is the "second landmark" to which Brint refers? Why did Adam lie to Amy during this incident? How does Adam react to Brint's questioning about it?
5. How does Adam explain finding two birth certificates?

Questions for Discussion:

1. What do you think caused the personality of Adam's mother to change radically?
2. Recall the incident when Adam acted upon his suspicions and looked at his father's secret papers. What did Adam do after making extraordinary discoveries? What alternative actions might he have taken? Do you think he acted in the best way? What would you have done?
3. Why do you think Adam has two birth certificates?

Writing Activity:

Have you ever looked at secret papers or investigated a place where you had been warned not to go? Write about such a real or imaginary event in your life. Be sure to use descriptive language that will give your writing a sense of mystery and suspense.

PAGES 67 – 86

Vocabulary: Word analogies are equations in which the first pair of words has the same relationship as the second pair of words. For example, HOT is to COLD as LOVE is to HATE. Both pairs of words are opposites. Choose the best word from the Word Box to complete each of the following analogies.

```
                      WORD BOX
   admonish      solicitous        wary
   decrepit      sustenance
```

1. REVEAL is to OBSCURE as PRAISE is to _____.

2. FILM is to RECREATION as BREAD is to _____.

3. NONCHALANT is to CARELESS as CONCERNED is to _____.

4. ANXIOUS is to NERVOUS as CAUTIOUS is to _____.

5. SHIRT is to THREADBARE as SHACK is to _____.

Questions:

1. Why doesn't Adam talk to Amy about his doubts? Do you think he should? Explain.

2. What does Adam discover about his mother's special telephone hour?

3. How does Martha respond when Adam's mother imagines the safety and peace of Martha's surroundings? Where might Martha be?

4. How have Adam's parents lied to him? How does Adam feel when he becomes aware of the lie?

5. Why do the three young men try to provoke a fight with Adam? Do you think he handles the situation well? What would you have done?

6. How much time passes between the end of the long session and Adam's sudden waking from sleep? What does he do when he awakens? Why do you think he does this?

7. What effect does Adam's comment about pills and needles have on Brint? Does Adam take any more pills that night?

Writing Activity:

Have you ever been caught in a lie or have you ever caught a friend or relative in a lie? Write about the incident, telling what you discovered and how you reacted.

Pages 67 – 86 (cont.)

Forming Hypotheses:

This is a good point to evaluate what you have learned so far and to form hypotheses about the true nature of the characters in the story.

Adam ⟨ Do you think Adam will reach his destination?

Why do you think he is being questioned?

[ ]

Brint ⟨ Do you think Adam should trust Brint?

Why do you think he is questioning Adam?

[ ]

Father ⟨ Why do you think Adam's father is in Rutterburg, Vermont?

Who do you think is pursuing him?

[ ]

Mother ⟨ Why does Adam's mother seem nervous and frightened?

Why do you think she didn't tell Adam about Aunt Martha?

[ ]

Amy ——— Why do you think Adam cannot reach Amy by telephone?

[ ]

PAGES 87 – 106

Vocabulary: Antonyms are words with opposite meanings. Draw a line from each word in column A to its antonym in column B. Then use the words in column A to fill in the blanks in the sentences below.

A	B
1. pockmarked	a. continue
2. suspend	b. retreats
3. uninhabited	c. untie
4. lash	d. sink
5. soar	e. smooth
6. approaches	f. occupied

. . . .

1. As soon as we released the helium balloon, we watched it _____ into the sky.

2. We will _____ the investigation now, and continue it after the weekend.

3. The railroad gate will block the track as the train _____.

4. I will _____ the package to my bike after you untie it from yours.

5. The house appeared to be _____ until I got close and saw that it was occupied by a family of mice.

6. The girl with the _____ skin envied her sister's smooth complexion.

Pages 87 – 106 (cont.)

Questions:

1. How does Adam's mood change during the moments before and after he tries to call Amy? Why are his cheeks wet as he escapes from the troublemakers?

2. Compare Adam's mood as he begins to tell Brint about the gray man and his mood at the end of the session. How can you explain the change?

3. Why does Adam think he should have taken his pills? What three options does he explore while being chased? Does he have others? Why does he continue on his ride?

4. How does Brint respond to Adam on the day following the session when Adam remained silent?

Questions for Discussion:

1. After a day of refusing to get out of bed, why do you think Adam remains silent during a short session with Brint? What do you think is bothering Adam?

2. Why do you think Adam doesn't tell the old man and his wife the truth about his fall?

Writing Activity:

Write about a time in real life or in a dream when you believed you were being chased by someone who wanted to harm you. Tell whether you understood why you were being pursued and describe your emotions at the time.

PAGES 107 – 135

Vocabulary: Draw a line from each word on the left to its meaning on the right. Then use the numbered words to fill in the blanks in the sentences below.

1. appalled   a. horrified

2. desecrate   b. absorbed

3. subterfuge   c. so small it may be disregarded

4. assimilated   d. without originality

5. idyllic   e. charmingly simple; peaceful

6. indict   f. damage; treat with sacrilege

7. negligible   g. accuse to initiate a criminal case

8. banal   h. deception to hide something

. . . .

1. Without sufficient evidence, the Grand Jury failed to _____ the robbery suspect.

2. The smokestacks of the steel mill interrupted an otherwise _____ country landscape.

3. The degree of error is so small as to be _____.

4. Jack was so _____ by his brother's rude behavior that he pretended not to know him at all.

5. She found that far from being witty, his conversation was quite _____.

6. The espionage agent surrendered because he was tired of his life of _____.

7. The police stopped the graffiti artist who tried to _____ the church walls with pictures and slogans.

8. Within two generations, most immigrant groups become _____ into American society.

Pages 107 – 135 (cont.)

Questions:

1. Why does Adam awaken in pain? How does Brint explain the measures taken?

2. What does Adam learn about Mr. Grey's identity? How does this differ from what Adam has been told?

3. What does Adam's father finally reveal about Paul Delmonte? Why does he tell Adam now?

4. Why does Adam once again become uneasy about Brint's motives?

5. What information does Adam say his father never revealed? Do you believe Adam or do you think he is withholding information from Brint? How does he explain his father's secrecy about this information?

6. Why was the Department of Re-Identification developed? Does such a government department actually exist today?

7. Why was Adam's father's life in danger? What finally convinced him to go into hiding? What were his other options?

Questions for Discussion:

1. Do you think Adam's father should have revealed his identity to his son sooner?

2. Do you think Adam's suspicions are justified or do you believe Brint's explanation for his own impatience?

3. How does Brint refer to the end of each session? What other terms might he use? Why do you think he uses these terms?

4. Do you think you could live comfortably with a changed identity under the Witness Protection Program? What would life be like? What might you need to guard against?

Writing Activity:

Based upon what you have learned about Adam's past and about his relationship with Brint, predict what will happen in the climax (turning point in the plot). You might include what happens when Adam gets to Rutterburg and how Adam ends up in the sanitarium.

PAGES 136 – 151

Vocabulary: Use the context to determine the best meaning for the underlined word in each of the following sentences. Circle the letter of the answer you choose.

1. We were <u>dumbfounded</u> as we watched the magician pull a live rabbit from his hat.
   a. silent   b. astonished   c. aggravated   d. provoked

2. The <u>massive</u> hippopotamus must enjoy floating in the river, where its bulky body can get some relief from the heat.
   a. obsolete   b. miniature   c. unattractive   d. huge

3. When he gets angry, he often becomes <u>melodramatic</u>, shouting and gesturing wildly.
   a. exaggerated in   b. shy and unable   c. persistant to an   d. troubled;
   tone and sentiment   to act   annoying degree   fearful

4. The entire job was so boring that she decided to do it in a <u>piecemeal</u> fashion over several days.
   a. relaxed   b. gradual   c. cautious   d. tense

5. Her <u>wistful</u> expression as she wrote the letter revealed how much she missed him.
   a. tragic   b. indifferent   c. yearning   d. gleeful

6. She <u>recoiled</u> in disgust when she saw the wolf attack the sheep.
   a. shrank back   b. jumped forward   c. stood still   d. ran fast

Questions:

1. What do you think is the obese man's relationship to the man inside the apartment? What prompts the obese man to tell Adam where his bike can be found?

2. How does Adam feel about his father when he discovers what his father has done? How would you feel?

3. How does Adam's father feel about Mr. Grey? How are these feelings similar to those that Adam has about Brint?

4. Why is Adam dependent upon Brint?

5. What does Adam discover about his aunt's sheltered living situation? Why do you think Adam's mother was allowed to continue their telephone relationship? What other questions raised earlier in the novel are now answered?

Pages 136 – 151 (cont.)

Questions for Discussion:

How do you think the move affected each member of Adam's family? Whom do you think the move hurt most? Who was affected the least? Do you think the family should have made the move?

Writing Activities:

1. Write about a real or imagined time when you and your family had to make a sudden move to a new location. Describe the reasons for the move, tell what possessions could be taken along, and indicate how each family member felt about the move.

2. Imagine you are Adam and you are able to write a letter to your father. In this letter pose all of the questions about your life that are still unanswered.

PAGES 152 – 168

Vocabulary: Draw a line from each word on the left to its meaning on the right. Then use the numbered words to fill in the blanks in the sentences below.

1. consumed
2. paranoid
3. contemptuous
4. afflicted
5. quizzically
6. alcove
7. remnant

a. scornful; showing disdain
b. recess or small room adjacent to a large room
c. remainder
d. in a questioning or puzzling manner
e. devoured; exhausted
f. severely distressed
g. excessively suspicious of others

. . . .

1. Raised in an atmosphere of prejudice and bigotry, Anne was _____ of people of different racial backgrounds.

2. A series of anonymous telephone calls made me _____ about answering the phone and going out after dark.

3. After burning for two weeks, the fire had _____ the entire forest.

4. The dog looked at his master _____ when he gestured toward the open door.

5. Place your bed into the _____ of your studio apartment to take advantage of the space you have.

6. The winter was so harsh it seemed as if everyone was _____ with the flu.

7. As he got ready for college, he threw away every _____ of his high school days.

Questions:

1. What were the "Never Knows"?

2. What does Adam mean when he recalls that "Somehow fear had forged love"?

3. What are Adam's unspoken thoughts when Amy asks him if anything is "bugging" him?

4. What do you think Adam means when he says he threw away the aspirin because he "didn't want to be found with pills on [him]"?

5. What aspects of Adam's experience on his bike ride to Rutterburg parallel references made during the taped sessions with Brint?

Pages 152 – 168 (cont.)

Literary Element: Plot

The plot of a novel refers to a series of events in the order they are told. What are the two parallel plots that seem to be operating in this novel so far?

Plot #1

_____

_____

_____

_____

_____

_____

Plot #2

_____

_____

_____

How do you think these plots relate to each other?

_____

_____

_____

Writing Activities:

1. Write about a time when a shared feeling of fear or joy drew you and a family member or friend closer together.
2. Write about a dream you have had that was so realistic that you thought the events were really happening. Explain how circumstances or events in your waking life might have triggered the dream.

PAGES 169 – 192

Vocabulary: Choose the best word from the Word Box to complete each of the following analogies.

<table>
<tr><td colspan="3" align="center">*WORD BOX*</td></tr>
<tr><td>reiterate</td><td>sporadically</td><td>wan</td></tr>
<tr><td>responsive</td><td>turbulent</td><td></td></tr>
</table>

1. ALWAYS is to OCCASIONALLY as REGULARLY is to _____.
2. FURNISH is to REFURNISH as STATE is to _____.
3. HAPPY is to EXUBERANT as MELANCHOLY is to _____.
4. DISCONTENTED is to SATISFIED as CALM is to _____.
5. GENEROUS is to MONEY as _____ is to WORDS.

Questions:

1. Compare Adam's impressions of the doctor who gives him shots with his feelings about Brint. How has Adam's relationship with Brint changed?
2. When Adam chooses not to return to his room for a rest, he explains, "At least here, I know I exist." What do you think he means?
3. Why does Adam avoid Amy? If you were Adam, would you avoid her?
4. How do Amy and Adam carry out the church parking lot "Number"? How does Adam feel about participating in it?
5. What is referred to as the "nightmare [that] had already started . . . without him"?
6. On what two previous occasions had the family taken "vacations" because of the possibility that their cover had been blown? Where will they go now?
7. As Adam pedals toward the motel, remembering a family trip there, how long does he believe it has been since he stayed there? How long does the attendant say the motel has been closed? What might explain the discrepancy?
8. What happens when Adam tries to call Amy again? How long does the man at the other end of the phone say he has had his current number?
9. Why does Adam scream and faint? What language does he use to describe his own reactions?

Writing Activity:

Imagine you are Adam. Write a journal entry after you realize that you have lost track of two or three years of your life. Indicate what you are sure about, what you still need to know to fill in the pieces of the puzzle, and what you are feeling as you write.

PAGES 193 – 213

Vocabulary: Draw a line from each word on the left to its definition on the right. Then use the numbered words to fill in the blanks in the sentences below.

1. subdued		a.	wander aimlessly
2. antiseptic		b.	great destruction
3. reminiscing		c.	recalling past experiences
4. meander		d.	quiet or controlled
5. mottled		e.	cannot be proven wrong
6. irrefutable		f.	spotted or blotched
7. holocaust		g.	exceptionally clean or neat

. . . .

1. Faced with _____ evidence, he stopped arguing.

2. It is pleasant to _____ through the woods on a cool, spring day.

3. A ripe banana has a(n) _____ skin.

4. Many people fear a nuclear _____ if nations cannot agree to arms control.

5. The brightly-colored posters help to offset the _____ look of the doctor's waiting room.

6. Although many people expected her to wail and sob, Abby was quiet and _____ when she heard about the tragedy.

7. They enjoyed _____ about their senior year at their ten-year high school reunion.

Questions:

1. How do the season and weather at the start of the family trip compare with the season and weather described at the outset of Adam's bike trip?

2. What is the similarity between the description of the car crashing into Adam's family and the earlier description of the car with the three young men forcing Adam's bike into the ditch?

3. Who makes the observation, "They'll get him—they never miss"? Who are "they"? Who won't get away? Does Adam tell Brint who spoke these words?

4. What does Adam see when he finally reaches Rutterburg on his bike? What did he see on a hill when he started out from Monument?

Pages 193 – 213 (cont.)

5. Who is Dr. Dupont? What is the significance of the words, "He is always waiting for me"?

6. Why does Adam say, while looking through the gates, "Someday I will ride out there"? Has he been beyond the gates? If not, how do you think he discovered such details as the fact that the motel has been closed for three years?

7. Why do you think Adam knows his mother is dead, but still has hope for his father? Might Adam's father be alive? What is the significance of the line ". . .we talk about my father and I find out again that he is dead"?

8. What is the significance of Adam's father's jacket and cap? Why do you think Brint brought them to the sanatorium?

9. What is File Data 865-01? Who is Personnel #2222? Witness #599-6?

10. How often does the questioning occur, at what intervals, and why?

11. What is Policy 979 and why is one advisory being advanced to eliminate it? What are the other two advisories?

12. What does the report reveal about Mr. Grey?

13. Why is Adam a problem, and for whom?

14. Why is the final page a repetition of the first page of the book? What does this suggest about Adam's future?

Novel Coincidences:

As the novel comes to an end, the characters and events of Adam's bike ride reappear in slightly altered forms at the hospital. Draw a line from the description on the left to its corresponding character on the right.

Bike Ride	**Hospital**
1. kind man at the gas station who helped Adam	a. Silver
2. three "wise guys" who took Adam's package and threw him into a ditch	b. Junior Varney
3. threatening dog in the road	c. Mr. Harvester
4. obese man	d. Arthur
5. boy who stole Adam's bike	e. Luke
6. restaurant owner who served Adam chowder while chatting on the telephone	f. Whipper, Dobie, and Lewis

Pages 193 – 213 (cont.)

Literary Element: Theme

The theme of a work of literature refers to its underlying ideas, its message or the author's purpose in writing the story. In *I Am the Cheese*, what is Cormier saying about the power of the individual within a bureaucratic society? What comment is he making about authority figures within our society? What happens to the individual who stands up to corruption and tries to fight back?

Literary Devices:

I. *Irony*—A situation is considered ironic when it represents a twist of fate or presents an outcome that is the opposite of what is expected. Explain the meaning of the title of the novel. What is ironic about it? What is the central irony of the book concerning Adam's bike ride?

II. *Foreshadowing*—In a well-constructed novel of mystery or suspense the author foreshadows the ending or provides clues in advance of the outcome. Did you realize in advance of the ending that Adam's journey never took him outside the hospital? Were you surprised at the ending? What clues did the author provide to foreshadow the conclusion?

Writing Activity:

Write about a real or fictional time when you stood up to a figure of authority or you "blew the whistle" on an unfair or illegal practice. Describe the circumstance that you contested and tell about the consequences of your rebellion.

CLOZE ACTIVITY

The following passage is taken from page three of the novel. Read the entire passage. Then go back and fill in each blank with one word that makes sense in the passage. Afterwards, you may compare your language with that of the author.

I went to the cabinet in the den and took out the gift for my father. I wrapped it

in _____[1] foil and then wrapped it again with _____,[2]

Scotch-taping it all securely. Then I went _____[3] to the cellar and got the

pants _____[4] shoes and jacket, but it took me _____[5] least a

half hour to find the _____.[6] But I found it: the cap I _____,[7]

my father's old cap. It would be _____[8] on the road to Vermont and

_____[9] cap is perfect, woolen, the kind that I could _____[10]

over my ears if the cold became a _____.[11]

Then I raided my savings. I have _____[12] of money. I have

thirty-five _____[13] and ninety-three cents. I have enough money to

_____[14] first class to Vermont, in the Greyhound _____[15]

that goes all the way to Montreal, _____[16] I know that I am going by

_____[17] to Rutterburg, Vermont. I don't want to be _____[18]

to a bus. I want the open _____[19] before me, I want to sail on the

_____.[20] The bike was waiting in the garage _____[21] that's

how I wanted to go. By bike, by my own strength and power. For my father.

POST-READING ACTIVITIES

1. An epilogue is a short section added to the end of a novel. Typically, it tells what happens to the characters after the events in the story. Write a one-page epilogue in the form of "T's" next annual report.

2. To better understand the effect of varying points of view, prepare and present one-minute monologues for Adam and each of his parents. Choose any single event in the story that has dramatic appeal, and that affects all three characters.

3. The family's disappearance from Blount was explained by a car accident. Write a headline and news story that contain the explanation for the family's disappearance from Monument. Include a captioned picture of the family, using a sketch, photo, or magazine cut-out.

4. Suppose you are Adam's father and you have escaped your killers. Write a letter to Adam a year after the accident. Discuss whether you would testify if you had it to do again. What other options might you have exercised? Would any other decision have been "moral"?

5. Design a book jacket for *I Am the Cheese* by cutting a piece of paper to fit the opened book, folded twice to overlap each cover. Include a plot summary on the inside front cover and a captivating front cover illustration. On the inside back cover write a paragraph about the author and list other books he has written.

6. In the novel Adam refers to the writer Thomas Wolfe with admiration. How does the title of Wolfe's most famous novel, *You Can't Go Home Again*, reflect Adam's condition?

7. Pretend that you are Mr. Grey. Write a letter to your superior explaining why you feel your suspension should be discontinued. Explain your actions on the night of the murder. Attach a resume summarizing relevant biographical data and a history of your job service.

8. Rewrite a short episode from the novel in dialogue form and record it as a radio play on tape or as a drama on video. Include sound effects and background music consistent with the mood of the novel.

9. Find examples in newspaper and magazine stories about people who have been "whistler-blowers" and have been placed in government witness protection programs. What dangers do these people face and why did they "blow the whistle"?

SUGGESTIONS FOR FURTHER READING

Bennett, Jay. *Say Hello the Hit Man*. Dell

* Bradbury, Ray. *Fahrenheit 451*. Ballantine.

_____. *Something Wicked This Way Comes*. Bantam.

* Christopher, John. *The White Mountains*. Simon & Schuster.

* Duncan, Lois. *Down a Dark Hall*. Dell.

* Guest, Judith. *Ordinary People*. Penguin.

Hemingway, Ernest. *To Have and Have Not*. Simon & Schuster.

* Hinton, S. E. *Rumble Fish*. Dell.

* Holman, Felice. *Slake's Limbo*. Simon & Schuster.

* Kesey, Ken. *One Flew Over the Cuckoo's Nest*. Penguin.

L'Engle, Madeleine. *Arm of the Starfish*. Dell.

* Lowry, Lois. *The Giver*. Dell.

* Orwell, George. *Animal Farm*. New American Library.

* _____. *1984*. New American Library.

* Sleator, William. *Interstellar Pig*. Dell.

* White, Robb. *Deathwatch*. Dell.

* Zindel, Paul. *The Pigman*. Dell.

Other Novels by Robert Cormier

After the First Death. Dell.

Beyond the Chocolate War. Dell.

The Bumblebee Flies Anyway. Dell.

* *The Chocolate War*. Dell.

Eight + One. Dell.

Fade. Dell.

A Little Raw on Monday Mornings. Dell.

Now and At the Hour. Dell.

Take Me Where the Good Times Are. Dell.

* NOVEL-TIES Study Guides are available for these titles.

ANSWER KEY

Pages 1 – 11

Vocabulary: 1. d 2. a 3. g 4. b 5. c 6. e 7. f ; 1. hesitantly 2. resolute 3. warped 4. momentum 5. omen 6. claustrophobic 7. retreated

Questions: 1. The story takes place in contemporary New England. The dreary fall weather parallels the narrator's anxiety. A burst of sunshine accompanies the narrator's surge of courageous recklessness. 2. It is clear that the narrator is not taking an ordinary bike trip because he had not told anyone that he was leaving, he spills a bottle of pills, and refers to many fears. 3. "A" remembers overhearing a tense conversation between his parents when he was three years old, about what to do with him, and a long bus ride to a new home. He has memory gaps about life before the move and details afterward. He feels anxious about the memory gaps. Brint seems encouraging, but not pushy, after the pauses. 4. "A" does not totally trust Brint.

Pages 12 –24

Vocabulary: 1. g 2. f 3. d 4. b 5. c 6. a 7. e; 1. hurtling 2. administered 3. insignificant 4. obliterating 5. raucously 6. impaled 7. vulnerable

Questions: 1. The narrator stops at the gas station to rest, ask for a map, and check the air in his tires. 2. "A" will not discuss Delmonte and Amy Hertz. Brint seems sympathetic and unintrusive. 3. The narrator's song is comforting because it reminds him of singing with his father while snuggling in his mother's lap. 4. While bicycling, the narrator recalls childhood nameplay with his father about "Adam Farmer." 5. Adam is glad he did not take the pills because they would mar his alertness and spoil his enjoyment of the day.

Pages 25 – 43

Vocabulary: 1. askew–crooked 2. futile–useless 3. camaraderie–friendship 4. marooned–isolated 5. apparition–ghost

Questions: 1. The dog on the highway is a ferocious German shepard that tries to overturn the bicyclist. Adam escapes when the dog is distracted by a car. In the woods, Adam and his father are threatened by a small, crazed dog. Adam's father attacked the dog while Adam retreated. 2. When Adam asks about Brint and the hospital, Brint is evasive, returning question for question. 3. Adam decides that although he has no reason to distrust Brint, he will be clever and careful about what he divulges. Adam decides to provide some information so that he can be in control. 4. After the encounter with the dog, Adam sees his father as a courageous individual. For the first time he is able to think about him objectively. 5. When Adam reaches Howard Johnson's, he is fatigued, hungry, and discouraged. He feels the need to talk to Amy. 6. Adam refers to an endless walk to the phone booth and indicates that he has lost all track of time.

Pages 44 – 66

Vocabulary: 1. c 2. d 3. a 4. d 5. b

Questions: 1. Adam says that Amy loves mischief but has her serious moments, likes books, is blue-eyed, short, robust, freckled, and buxom. 2. According to Adam, his mother is now subdued, tense, withdrawn, and nervous. She was once a "laughing, tender woman." 3. The first "Number" involves filling and then abandoning supermarket shopping carts. Adam has mixed feelings about his own participation, but loves to watch Amy. 4. The second landmark is the call from Amy about visiting the editor from Rawlings, supposedly Adam's hometown. The memory of a flight he took when he was a young child prompted Adam to lie to Amy. When Brint encourages Adam to elaborate, he says he is tired and doesn't want to talk. 5. Adam rationalizes his two birth certificates by assuming the town clerk made an error and had to make up a new birth certificate.

Pages 67 – 86

Vocabulary: 1. admonish 2. sustenance 3. solicitous 4. wary 5. decrepit

Questions: 1. Adam does not talk to Amy about his doubts because he is afraid she would laugh at him or think less of him. Answers to the second part of the question will vary. 2. Adam discovers that his mother talks regularly to Martha, Adam's aunt. 3. Martha gently scolds Adam's mother when she refers longingly to the serenity of her surroundings. Answers to the second part of the question will vary. 4. Adam's parents falsely told him that he had no relatives. Adam is horrified and angry when he discovers the lie. 5. Adam thinks the boys are looking for a fight simply because they are bored and they are bullies. Answers to the rest of the question will vary. 6. Adam wakes up at 2:15 the next morning, probably more than twelve hours after the

last session. Adam awakens in a panic about his identity and probably summons Brint to help him "fill in blanks." 7. Brint says that it may be a good sign that Adam is tired of pills and shots, but offers them twice; Adam ends by saying he will take a pill.

Pages 87 – 106

Vocabulary: 1. e 2. a 3. f 4. c 5. d 6. b; 1. soar 2. suspend 3. approaches 4. lash 5. uninhabited 6. pockmarked

Questions: 1. Adam is hopeful before the call, but upset and frightened afterwards. His wet cheeks indicate he has been crying. 2. Adam is excited at first. He becomes upset and angry as Brint presses for more information. Answers to the second part of the question will vary. 3. Adam thinks he should have taken the pills because they help him feel less lonely and panicky. Adam considers hiding in the fields, staying where he is, or riding on. Answers as to other possible options will vary. Adam continues to ride so that he will not have to abandon his bike or be hit. 4. Brint seems cheerful, sympathetic, and ready to wait for Adam to reveal what he knows.

Pages 107 – 135

Vocabulary: 1. a 2. f 3. h 4. b 5. e 6. g 7. c 8. d; 1. indict 2. idyllic 3. negligible 4. appalled 5. banal 6. subterfuge 7. desecrate 8. assimilated

Questions: 1. Adam awakens in pain because he was given several injections as a result of his silence. 2. Adam learns that Mr. Grey is not a supervisor in his father's insurance company, as he had been told, but actually "Mr. Thompson," a federal agent in the U.S. Department of Re-Identification. 3. Adam's father reveals that Adam was born "Paul Delmonte." His name was changed along with everyone else's in the family when Adam's father testified about government corruption. The family then went into hiding. His father thinks he is old enough to know now, especially since he is beginning to ask questions about his identity. 4. Brint becomes impatient, and Adam wonders again whether Brint really wants to help him or just wants to learn specific facts. 5. Adam says his father was not precise about the information he gave as testimony and about what he told Adam because he feared that this information might be dangerous for Adam. 6. The department was developed to provide new identities for witnesses whose testimony placed them in danger. The FBI actually has a witness protection program. 7. Adam's father's life was in danger because the mob might try to kill him to set an example to informers. Also, corrupt government officials may fear that he will incriminate them in the future. A threatening phone call to Adam's mother convinced the family to go into hiding. Answers to the last part of the question will vary, but may include the ideas that he could have tried his luck with a security guard or moved his family without consulting the authorities.

Pages 136 – 151

Vocabulary: 1. b 2. d 3. a 4. b 5. c 6. a

Questions: 1. Answers to the first part of the question will vary, but might include the idea that the other man is his lover or a caretaker. The obese man tells Adam the location of his bike because the man inside directs him to tell. 2. Adam is proud of his father when he finds out what he has done. Answers to the second part of the question will vary. 3. Adam's father dislikes Mr. Grey probing for information. Like Adam in his talks with Brint, Adam's father sometimes feels he and Mr. Grey are enemies. 4. Adam is dependent upon Brint for his help in remembering his past and coping with panic attacks by providing medication. 5. Adam learns that his aunt is a nun living in a convent. Adam's mother was able to continue their telephone relationship because she would not expect her sister to visit or share their conversations with anyone else. Therefore, Adam's aunt does not threaten their cover. Answers to the last part of the question will vary, but should include the following ideas: Adam's father gave up smoking after his identity change, Adam's mother was sad on the bus trip because the family was fleeing.

Pages 152 – 168

Vocabulary: 1. e 2. g 3. a 4. f 5. d 6. b 7. c; 1. contemptuous 2. paranoid 3. consumed 4. quizzically 5. alcove 6. afflicted 7. remnant

Questions: 1. The "Never Knows" were what Adam's mother referred to as the terrors about possible discovery. 2. Adam means that his family grew closer out of shared fear for their lives. 3. When Amy asks Adam if anything is "bugging" him, Adam thinks of how his home may be "bugged." 4. Answers will vary, but may include the idea that Adam fears that if he were picked up by police, aspirin might be confused with illicit drugs. 5. "I am a spy" is evocative of the subterfuge Adam describes during his sessions. Earlier, Adam is attacked by a dog who chases him back; Adam describes the dog attack in the woods to Brint.

Pages 169 – 192

Vocabulary: 1. sporadically   2. reiterate   3. wan   4. turbulent   5. responsive

Questions: 1. Adam feels that the doctor who gives him the shots is kind. While at first Adam believed that Brint might be trying to help him fill in memory gaps, Adam now distrusts Brint and suspects his motives. 2. Although Adam escapes the anxiety brought on by questioning when he is outside the room with bars, he prefers the tension inside the room where he is interrogated to the blissful oblivion he experiences outside when he is drugged. 3. Adam avoids Amy because he is afraid he will reveal the truth to her. Answers to the second part of the question will vary. 4. While people are inside the church at a wedding, Amy and Adam sneak into their cars and turn on the radios and windshield wipers. Adam is hesitant about breaking into cars, but does not want to disappoint Amy. 5. The nightmare is that the family's cover has been blown. 6. Prior occasions when the family "vacationed" occurred when TV crews came to document the town's bicentennial and when a congressional witness mentioned a newspaperman informant somewhat like Adam's father. Now they will go north to a motel in New England. 7. Adam believes his family stayed in the cabin a year ago. The attendant says the motel has been closed for two or three years. Answers to the last part of the question will vary. 8. When Adam calls Amy, an irritated man says he has had the number for three years. 9. Adam realizes that his perception of reality is faulty. His memories of when he last visited the motel and when he talked to Amy are three years out of date. Adam describes his reactions as if he is dissociated from them. He says that "a terrible sound fills my ears" as he describes his own screams.

Pages 193 – 213

Vocabulary: 1. d   2. g   3. c   4. a   5. f   6. e   7. b; 1. irrefutable   2. meander   3. mottled   4. holocaust   5. antiseptic   6. subdued   7. reminiscing

Questions: 1. Both trips begin on muted October days. 2. There are similarities in the descriptions of helplessness, glinting steel, twisting, and a release into unconsciousness. The attack was planned, as the harassment by the boys in the car had been, and just as inescapable. 3. Grey is talking about the inevitability of Adam's father's capture by the assassins who are probably members of organized crime. Adam does not reveal to Brint that he knows it was Grey who spoke. 4. When he reaches Rutterburg, Adam sees the hospital, just as he saw a hospital at the outset. 5. Dr. Dupont is the psychiatrist who administers Adam's shots. The bike trip actually took place within the perimeter of the sanatorium; the doctor is an ever-present part of Adam's life. 6. Until now, Adam has really not left the gates. Answers about his discoveries will vary. Perhaps during one of his moments of lucidity, Adam realizes that if he were to return to the motel, he might find that it had closed since his last visit three years ago. 7. Adam saw his dead mother, but never saw his father's body. The final tape transcript, however, confirms the "termination of the witness." Adam "finds out again" because he is questioned to the point of remembering the murder every year. 8. Adam had mentioned his mother's revelation that she had kept her husband's cap and jacket against orders to destroy evidence of their past. Answers to the second part of the question will vary. Brint probably arranged to have the items brought from Adam's home to the sanatorium to aid his memory. 9. File Data 865-01 is information about the Witness Re-Establishment Project. Personnel #2222 is Grey. Witness #599-6 is Adam's father. 10. Questioning occurs at twelve-month intervals, every day or so for about two weeks. The purpose is to find out if Adam knows more than he has revealed about his father's knowledge of corruption in government. 11. Policy 979 is a federal agency procedure prohibiting Department 1-R (the department seeking information from Adam) from killing individuals in its charge, such as Adam. If the procedure is changed so that such killing is <u>not</u> against policy, Adam can be killed. Any information he has that might interfere with mob influence on government would die with him. Advisory #2 is that Grey no longer be suspended, but be re-instated to his position in the agency. Advisory #3 is that the department should either keep Adam confined until policy is changed so that they can kill him, or keep him confined and medicated until he dies. 12. The report reveals that Grey probably contacted the assassins about the family's whereabouts. The implication is that Grey, a government agent, may have mob connections. After the murder, he had the bodies eliminated and had Adam sent to the confinement facility without local press attention. 13. Adam might be a problem for corrupt officials in power, whose mob connections he could reveal. 14. The final page is a restatement of the first paragraph of the book. This suggests that Adam will remain institutionalized and experience the same cycle of events (drug-influenced "bike ride," questioning, bringing up past memories, blurring them with medication, etc.) over and over again until he dies or is killed.

DATE DUE

WITHDRAWN